Master Math

SUPER CALCULATIONS

Numbers up to 100, calculations, and fractions

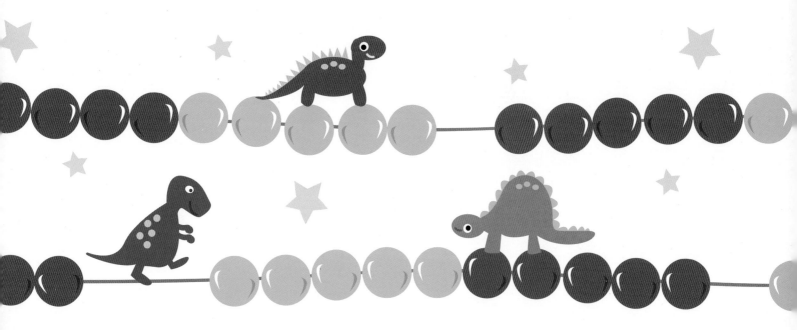

ANJANA CHATTERJEE   ILLUSTRATED BY JO SAMWAYS

CONSULTATION BY
RUTH BULL, BSc (HONS), PGCE, MA (ED)

Quarto is the authority on a wide range of topics.

Quarto educates, entertains and enriches the lives of our readers—enthusiasts and lovers of hands-on living.

www.quartoknows.com

Author: Anjana Chatterjee
Consultant: Ruth Bull, BSc (HONS), PGCE, MA (ED)
Designers: emojo design and Victoria Kimonidou
Illustrator: Jo Samways
Editors: Claire Watts and Ellie Brough

© 2018 Quarto Publishing plc
First Published in 2018 by The Quarto Library,
an imprint of The Quarto Group.
6 Orchard Road, Suite 100
Lake Forest, CA 92630
T: +1 949 380 7510
F: +1 949 380 7575
www.QuartoKnows.com

Distributed in the United States and Canada by
Lerner Publisher Services
241 First Avenue North
Minneapolis, MN 55401 U.S.A.
www.lernerbooks.com

A CIP record for this book is available at the Library of Congress.

ISBN 978 1 68297 320 2

9 8 7 6 5 4 3 2 1

Manufactured in DongGuan, China TL102017

FSC
www.fsc.org

MIX
Paper from
responsible sources
FSC® C104723

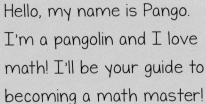

Hello, my name is Pango. I'm a pangolin and I love math! I'll be your guide to becoming a math master!

CONTENTS

HOW TO USE THE BOOKS IN THIS SERIES

The four books in Year 1 of the Master Math series focus on the main strands of the curriculum but using the leading Singapore math approach. This method involves teaching children to think and explain mathematically, with an emphasis on problem solving, focusing on the following three-step approach:

1 Concrete

Children engage in hands-on learning activities using concrete objects such as counters, cubes, dice, paper clips, or buttons. For example, children might add 4 cubes and 3 cubes together.

2 Pictorial

Children draw pictorial representations of mathematical concepts. For example, children might draw a number bond diagram showing that 3 and 4 together make 7.

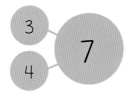

3 Abstract

Children can then move on to solving mathematical problems in an abstract way by using numbers and symbols. Once children understand that 3 and 4 make 7 when they are added together, they can use the abstract method to record it.

$$3 + 4 = 7$$

Each unit of the book begins with a question or statement that encourages children to begin thinking about a new mathematical concept. This is followed by visual explanations and hands-on activities that lead children to a deep conceptual understanding. Children should repeat and vary the activities, and be encouraged to revisit earlier sections to seek clarification and to deepen their understanding. You will find extension activities and further instruction in the Parent and Teacher Guidance sections.

It's time to look closely at numbers!

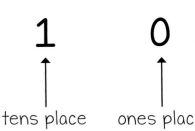

Let's think about the way we write numbers.
We're going to look at **place value**.

Look at the beads on the string.
Count how many beads there are.

There are 10 beads.
When we write the number ten, we use two **digits**.
We use 1 and 0.
We write 0 at the **ones place** and 1 at the **tens place**.
10 means 1 ten and 0 ones.

The word digit means any of the symbols that make the numbers from 0 to 9.
0, 1, 2, 3, 4, 5, 6, 7, 8, and 9 are numbers made with one digit.
10 is made with two digits.

1 0
tens place   ones plac

LOOKING AT ONES AND TENS

Let's think about how we write tens and ones.

How many beads are there altogether on this string? Count them.

There are 23 beads.

Now let's count using tens.

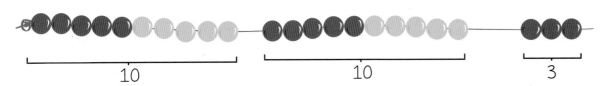

10   10   3

There are 2 tens. We write 2 in the tens place.
There are 3 ones. We write 3 in the ones place.
23 means 2 tens and 3 ones.

2 3

VOCABULARY: place value, digit, ones place, tens place

USING A TEN-FRAME

You can show each number up to ten using one **ten-frame**.

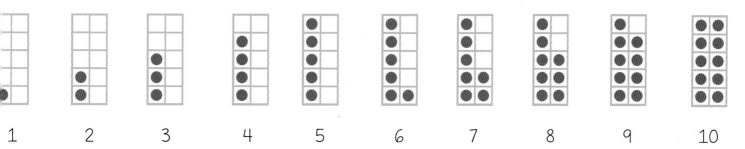

| 1 | 2 | 3 | 4 | 5 | 6 | 7 | 8 | 9 | 10 |

If you want to show numbers **greater** than ten, you need more than one ten-frame.

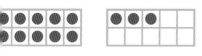

10   +   3   =   13

TRY THIS:

Can you say the numbers these ten-frames show?

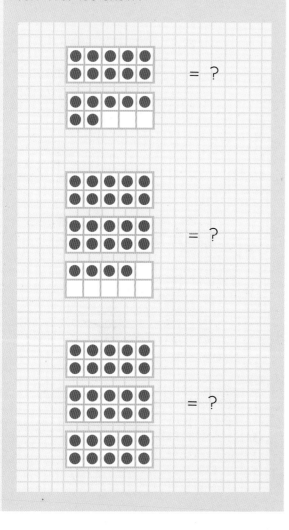

= ?

= ?

= ?

TRY THIS:

Try making these numbers using counters and ten-frames.

21   16   42
50   12   37

VOCABULARY: ten-frame, greater

INVESTIGATING TENS AND ONES

Let's look carefully at what tens and ones mean.

Look at the pencils.
There are 24 pencils.

We can show 24 like this.

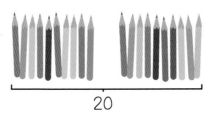  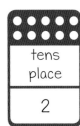

tens place	ones place
2	4

Look at the pencils.
There are 32 pencils.

We can show 32 like this.

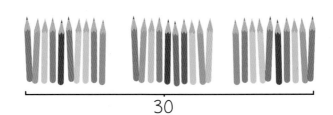 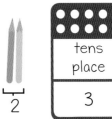

tens place	ones place
3	2

LET'S COMPARE

Compare 24 and 32. What is different?

24 has 2 tens and 4 ones.   32 has 3 tens and 2 ones.

To find out which number is greater, we look at the tens.
3 tens is greater than 2 tens.
32 is greater than 24.

VOCABULARY: compare

BEFORE, BETWEEN, AFTER

Let's look at the order of numbers.

Look at the vehicles at the traffic lights.

The bicycle comes **before** the car.

The car is **between** the bicycle and the van.

The van comes **after** the car.

Look at the number track.

| 1 | 2 | 3 | 4 | 5 | 6 | 7 | 8 | 9 | 10 | 11 | 12 | 13 | 14 | 15 | 16 | 17 | 18 | 19 | 20 | 21 | 22 | 23 | 24 | 25 | 26 | 27 | 28 | 29 | 30 |

Point to the number that comes before 9.
Point to the number that comes after 29.
Find 16 and 25. Point to a number that comes between 16 and 25.

TRY THIS:

Can you find the missing numbers in the sequences below?

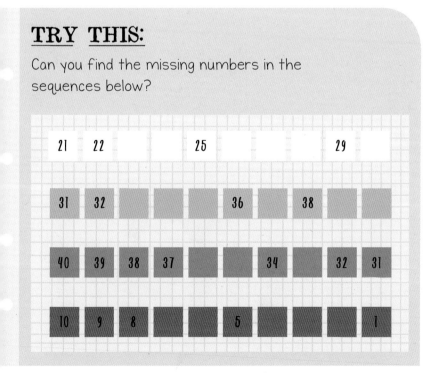

VOCABULARY: before, between, after

Let's compare the value of numbers and find out how to make them greater and **smaller** by adding and subtracting.

Remember that a number with two digits is **greater than** a number with only one digit.

When we add numbers the answer is greater. When we subtract numbers the answer is smaller.

22   >   9

22   is greater than   9

We use the sign **>** to show greater than.
It is easy to see that the 2-digit number is greater than the single-digit number.

Now let's compare two 2-digit numbers. Look at the tens place.

tens	ones
3	5

tens	ones
2	6

35   >   26

35   is greater than   26

3 tens is greater than 2 tens.
35 is greater than 26 because it has more tens.

But what do you do when the tens place is the same?

tens	ones
4	7

tens	ones
4	1

Look at the tens place.
There are 4 tens in 47. There are 4 tens in 41.
We need to compare the numbers at the ones place.
47 is greater than 41 because it has more ones.

47   >   41

47   is greater than   41

We can say this sentence in a different way.
We use the sign **<** to show **less than**.

41   <   47

41   is less than   47

COMPARE THREE 2-DIGIT NUMBERS

Look at the three numbers below.

24   36   40

Which is the **smallest** number?
Which is the **greatest** number?

PARENT AND TEACHER GUIDANCE

- Bundle small items, such as raisins or pasta shells, in groups of ten and put into small bags. These are the tens. Keep a group of ten items separate. These are the ones. Encourage your child to build numbers greater than ten using these items in tens and ones as concrete practice.

- Show how many tens there are in any two-digit number.

tens	ones
2	4

tens	ones
3	6

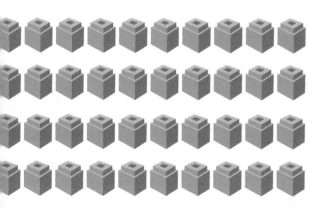

tens	ones
4	0

Look at the tens place of the three numbers.

2 tens < 3 tens

3 tens < 4 tens

So the smallest number is 24.

The greatest number is 40.

VOCABULARY: smallest, greatest

ADDING NUMBERS WITHIN 20

We can make numbers greater by adding them together. Let's practice!

ADDING WITH A NUMBER LINE

Look at the balloons.
Anna has 5 balloons. Niko gives her 8 balloons.
How many balloons does Anna have now?

We can use a number line to solve this problem.

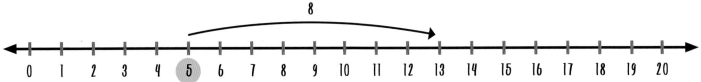

Anna has 5 balloons.
Start at 5.
Niko gives her 8 balloons.
Count on 8 places along the line.
Which number do you reach?
5 + 8 = 13

Remember that numbers become greater as you move along the number line this way.

TRY THIS:
Use a number line to solve this addition problem.
I have 10 whistles.
If I find another 4 whistles, how many whistles will I have altogether?

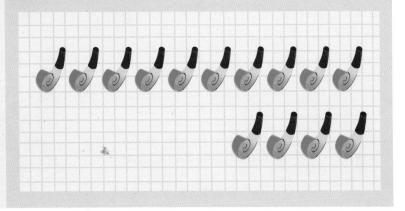

PARENT AND TEACHER GUIDANCE
- Remind children that it doesn't matter what order we add numbers in; the answer will be the same. Demonstrate with cubes or counters.

ADDING BY MAKING TEN

Let's try a different way of adding.

7 + 5 = ?

We can rearrange these cubes into tens and ones to work this out.

$$7 \qquad + \qquad 5$$

First, we break the 5 into 3 and 2.

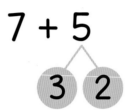

Add 3 cubes to the 7 cubes to make a ten.

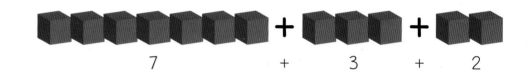

$$7 \qquad + \qquad 3 \qquad + \qquad 2$$

7 + 5 is the same as 10 + 2
7 + 5 = 12
10 + 2 = 12

$$10 \qquad + \qquad 2$$

THINKING ABOUT TEN

We can show the same problem with ten-frames.

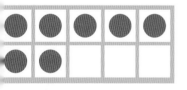
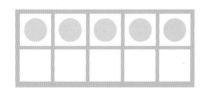

$$7 \qquad + \qquad 5$$

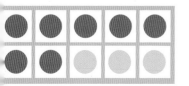
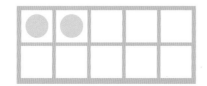

$$10 \qquad + \qquad 2$$

11

SUBTRACTING NUMBERS WITHIN 20

We can make numbers smaller by subtracting. Let's practice!

SUBTRACTING WITH A NUMBER LINE

There are 15 rabbits.

If 7 rabbits hop away, how many rabbits will be left?

We can use a number line to solve this problem.

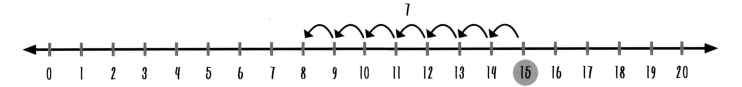

There are 15 rabbits.
Start at 15.
7 hop away.
Count back 7 places along the line.
Which number do you reach?
15 − 7 = 8

Remember that numbers become smaller as you move along the number line this way.

TRY THIS:

Use a number line to solve these subtraction problems.

There are 12 apples in the box.
If we eat 4 apples, how many are left?

There are 11 candies in the bowl.
If I eat 5 candies, how many are left?

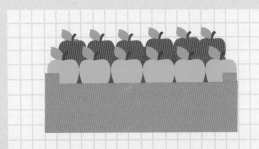

12

SUBTRACTING BY MAKING TEN

You can subtract by breaking larger numbers into tens and ones. We call this **partitioning**.

Look at the dinosaurs. Paul has 18 dinosaurs.

He gives 3 dinosaurs to Zak.
How many dinosaurs does Paul have left?

First, let's break 18 into tens and ones.

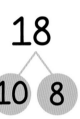

Now let's subtract the ones.
8 − 3 = 5

If Paul gives Zak 3 dinosaurs,
he has 10 dinosaurs and 5 dinosaurs left.

10 + 5 = 15

Paul has 15 dinosaurs left.

USING TEN-FRAMES

We can show the same problem with ten-frames.

Here is 18.

If we take away 3, the ten-frames
look like this.

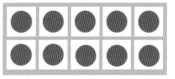
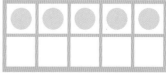
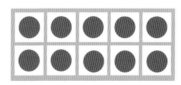

Multiplication is finding out how many there are altogether by thinking about **equal groups**. When we work out the total using groups, we are **multiplying**.

Equal groups means all the groups have to have the same number in them.

Here are 2 bags of apples.
Each bag has 5 apples each.

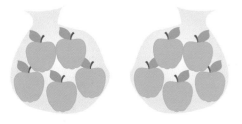

How many apples are there altogether?
We could count all the apples.

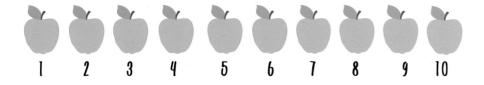

1 2 3 4 5 6 7 8 9 10

Or we could find out by making groups.
There are 2 groups of apples.
There are 5 apples in each group.

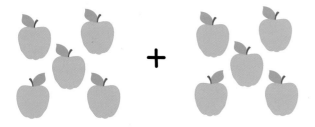

We write the numbers of each group and add them.
5 apples + 5 apples = 10 apples
2 groups of 5 apples make 10 altogether.

TRY THIS:

Hold up your hands and have your friend hold up her hands.
How many groups of fingers?
How many in each group?

4 groups with 5 fingers each.
5 + 5 + 5 + 5 = 20

VOCABULARY: multiplication, equal, group, multiply

Try thinking about these problems by multiplying.

There are 2 **lots of** books.

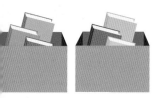

"Lots of" is another way of saying 'groups of'.

There are 3 books in each box.
How many books are there altogether?
Let's add 2 lots of 3 books.

+ 3 = 6

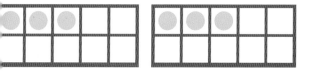

There are 6 books in total.

lots of 3 make 6.

Look at the bees.

Make 2 equal groups.

How many groups?
How many in each group?
groups of 2 make 4.

TRY THIS:

Can you find a way to group these crayons and add them? Remember, you need to have the same number of crayons in each group.

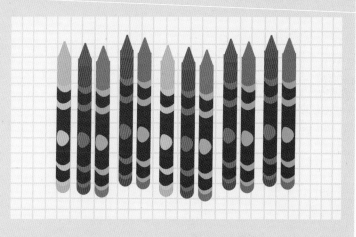

Now group the crayons in a different way and add them. What do you notice?

PARENT AND TEACHER GUIDANCE

- Talk about things that come in groups, such as 2 wings on a bird, 5 fingers on a hand, 8 legs on a spider. Go up to 12.

- As well as repeated addition, begin to count up in 2s, 5s, and 10s.

- Emphasize that when we multiply, each group must have the same number of objects.

MULTIPLICATION SENTENCES

Let's think about how we write multiplication problems.

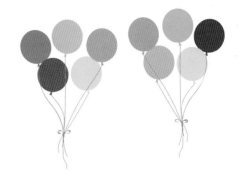

Look at the balloons.
There are 2 groups with 5 balloons each.

To find the total we add 5
and another 5.

There is another way to show this
addition sentence.
5 add 5 is the same as 2 groups of 5.

2 groups of 5

When we write a multiplication, we use the sign **x**. It means **multiplied by** or **times**.
We can write this **multiplication sentence**:
5 x 2 = 10

DOUBLING

When we multiply or times a number by 2, we say that we have **doubled** the number.
Double means times 2.

Double 4 is 8.

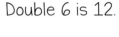

4 x 2 = 8

Double 6 is 12.

6 x 2 = 12

VOCABULARY: multiplied by, times, multiplication sentence, double 'hen you see a multiplication sentence, you can think of it as adding the same umber again and again. We call this **repeated addition**.

here are 4 bags of apples. Each bag has 6 apples.

hen we write 4 lots of 6 in a multiplication sentence, we write the 6 first.

x 4

his means 6 added 4 times.

apples and another 6 apples and another 6 apples and another 6 apples

+ 6 + 6 + 6 = 24

x 4 = 24

times 4 is 24.

multiplied by 4 is 24.

sixes are 24.

se cubes or counters to try out ese examples.

4 x 3 is the same as   4 + 4 + 4
                       4 multiplied by 3
                       3 lots of 4
                       3 fours

7 x 4 is the same as   7 + 7 + 7 + 7
                       7 multiplied by 4
                       4 lots of 7
                       4 sevens

TRY THIS:

Try turning these multiplication sentences into repeated additions.
Then figure out the answers.

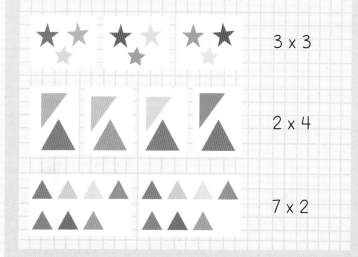

MULTIPLICATION CHALLENGE BOARD

Here's a multiplication game
for you to make and play.

1 Draw around the plate using a pencil.

2 Place the cup inside the circle you have
drawn and draw around it.

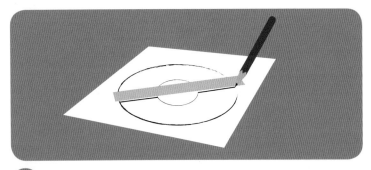

3 Ask an adult to help you draw lines to
split the larger circle into 10 sections.

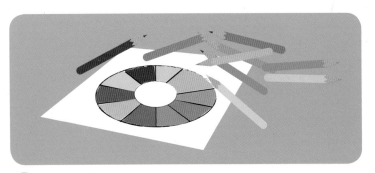

4 Color the sections of the larger circle
different colors.

YOU WILL NEED:

- a large sheet of thick paper
- 2 round objects of different
  sizes to draw around, such as
  a plate and a cup
- a pencil
- a ruler
- crayons
- scissors
- counters

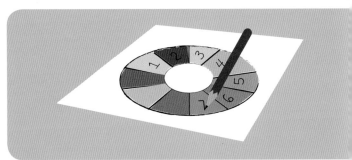

5 Write numbers 1 to 10 in each section
around the game board.

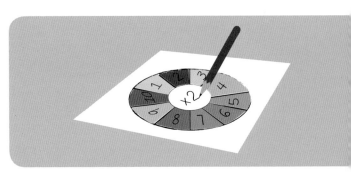

6 Write "x 2" in the small circle in
the center of the game board.

Ask an adult to help you cut out the game
board. To play the game, throw a counter
onto the board. When your counter lands
on a number, multiply it by 2.

MULTIPLICATION PROBLEMS

Let's think about multiplication problems. Follow the first
problem and then make up some problems of your own.

There are 3 sand castles on the beach.
Each sand castle has 4 flags.
How many flags are there altogether?

There are 3 sand castles with 4 flags each.
Write the addition sentence.

4 + 4 + 4 = 12

Now write the multiplication sentence.

4 x 3 = 12

There are 12 flags altogether.

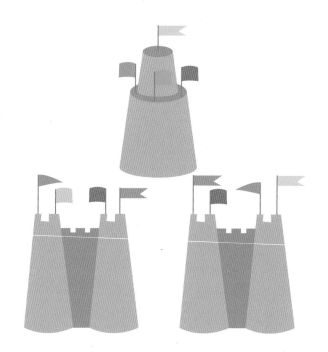

TRY THIS:

Look at the pictures.

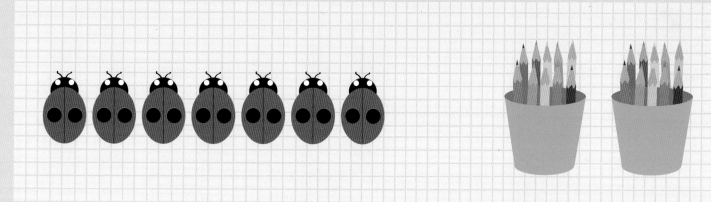

Make up a multiplication problem for each picture.
Write an addition sentence for your problem.
Write a multiplication sentence for your problem.

Now make up some multiplication problems of your own.

Use counters or cubes to help
you solve the problems.

19

Division is **sharing** things out or putting things into equal groups. When we share something equally, we are **dividing**.

Here are two examples of how things can be shared equally.

Here are 8 sandwiches.

2 children are going to share the sandwiches. Each child will have the same number of sandwiches.

When 8 sandwiches are shared equally between 2 children, each child will get 4 sandwiches.
8 **divided by** 2 is 4.

There are 9 cookies on the plate.

3 children are going to share the cookies.

When 9 cookies are shared equally between 3 children, each child will get 3 cookies.
9 divided by 3 is 3.

VOCABULARY: division, share, divide, divided by

SHARING GAME

When you share things equally, you are dividing. Here is a sharing game for you to play with a friend.

YOU WILL NEED:
- 6 paper plates
- 20 pretzel sticks
- a 1 – 6 spot die

1 Players take turns rolling the die. Look at the number on the top face of the die. Lay out the same number of plates.

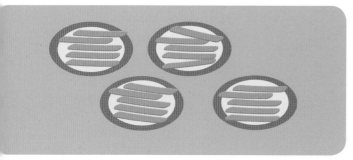

2 Share the pretzel sticks equally onto the plates.

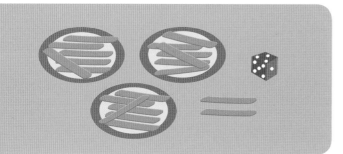

3 Sometimes, it will be impossible to share the pretzel sticks equally. There will be some **left over**. The player whose turn it is wins the leftover pretzel sticks and removes them from the game.

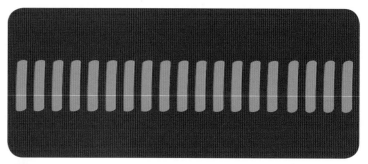

4 The next player counts the remaining pretzel sticks and the game continues with these pretzel sticks.

5 The game finishes when there are no pretzel sticks left to play with. The winner is the player with the most pretzel sticks.

PARENT AND TEACHER GUIDANCE
- Stress the fact that dividing means sharing into equal groups.

HOW MANY IN EACH GROUP?

Division means equal sharing.
When we share equally we can find out how many objects there are in a number of groups.

There are 12 triangles.

Put the triangles into 4 equal groups.

When we share 12 triangles into 4 groups, there are 3 triangles in each group.

If we share 12 equally into 4 groups, how many in each group?

4 groups of 3 divide equally into 12.

RABBITS AND CARROTS

Look at the carrots.

There are 6 carrots.

We need to share the carrots equally between 3 rabbits.

Put the carrots into 3 equal groups.
Each group will have 2 carrots.

If 6 carrots are shared equally between 3 rabbits, each rabbit gets 2 carrots.
We can write a division sentence to show this.
$6 \div 3 = 2$

When we write a **division sentence**, we use the sign ÷. It means divided by or shared by.

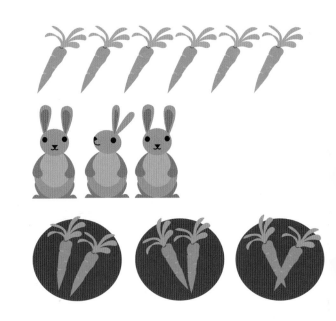

VOCABULARY: division sentence

When we share things equally, we find out how many groups contain an equal number of things. We use division to find out how many groups altogether.

There are 15 buttons.

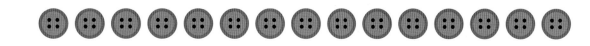

buttons fit on 1 shirt.

We can use grouping to find out how many shirts will use up all the buttons.

We have used 5 buttons but some are still left.

1 shirt

0 buttons fit on 2 shirts.

We have used 10 buttons but some are still left.

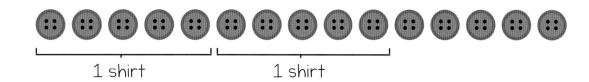

1 shirt   1 shirt

5 buttons fit on 3 shirts.

We have used all 15 buttons.
$15 \div 5 = 3$

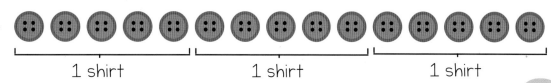

1 shirt   1 shirt   1 shirt

DIVIDE THE STARS

We can use cubes or counters to help solve division problems.

Can you divide these 8 stars into 2 equal groups?

Let's use cubes to solve this problem. Arrange 8 cubes in a line.

Share the cubes into 2 equal groups.

How many cubes are there in each group?

8 ÷ 2 = 4

So 8 divided by 2 is 4.

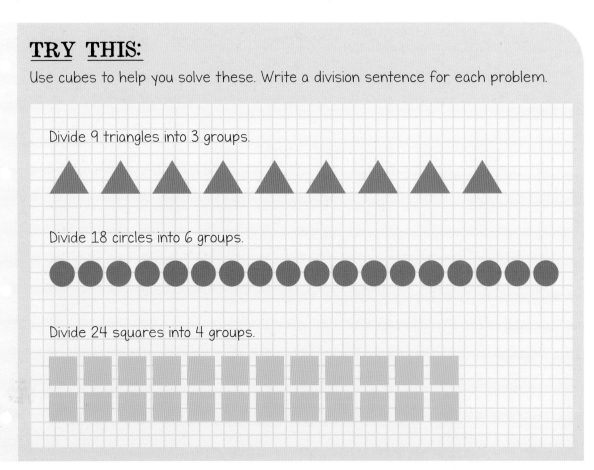

TRY THIS:
Use cubes to help you solve these. Write a division sentence for each problem.

Divide 9 triangles into 3 groups.

Divide 18 circles into 6 groups.

Divide 24 squares into 4 groups.

Let's look at some division problems.
Write a division sentence for each problem.

Nicola has 15 cars.

She shares them equally between 3 boxes.
How many cars will there be in each box?

There are 12 donuts.

You can fit 4 donuts in each box.
How many boxes do we need for all 12 donuts?

There are 12 carrots for 2 rabbits.
How many carrots will each rabbit get?

Now make up some division
problems of your own.

PARENT AND TEACHER GUIDANCE

- Children will soon come across numbers which cannot be divided evenly when they play division games or make up their own division problems. Talk about the amount "left over." Children may find it easier to understand this concept when they talk about sharing food or toys.

Let's look at some numbers that are smaller than one but bigger than zero.

Think about 1 of something.
For example, think about 1 apple.

What number is smaller than 1?

 1 apple

If I cut the apple into 2 equal pieces,
each piece is a **half** of the whole apple.
Equal means both the pieces are the same size.

When something is split into equal pieces, each piece is a **fraction** of the whole thing.
Half of an apple is a fraction of the whole apple.

TRY THIS:

These pictures show some things that have been cut into 2 pieces.
Some are halves and some are not.
Can you explain why?

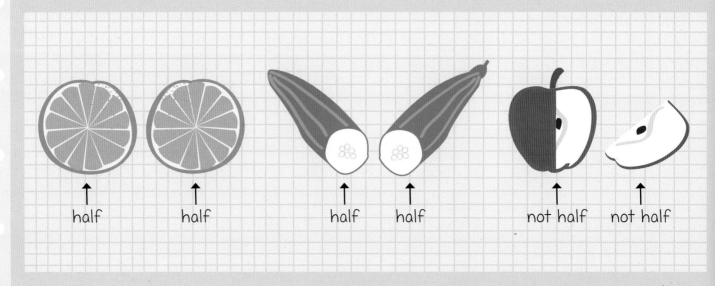

half   half   half   half   not half   not half

Let's look at another way of talking about and seeing halves.

Here are 8 cubes.

When we find half of a number of things, we put them into 2 equal groups.
We can find half of 8 by putting the cubes into 2 equal groups.

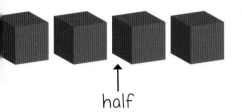

half

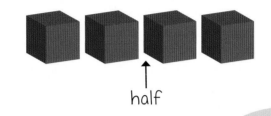

half

Half of 8 is 4.

We have split numbers into equal groups before.

We split numbers into equal groups when we were dividing.
When we find half of a number, we make 2 equal groups.
Finding half of a number is the same as dividing that number by 2.

8 ÷ 2 = 4

Do you remember? You can find out about dividing on pages 20 to 25.

TRY THIS:

Can you find half of these numbers of stars and triangles? Use cubes or counters to help you.

Write your answers in a sentence.
Half of 10 is ?
10 ÷ 2 = ?
When we write half as a number, we write it this way: ½.
½ of 10 is ?

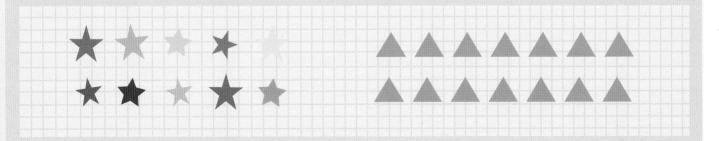

We can find half of something in another way.

This bottle is full of juice.

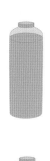

If we pour out all of the juice, it fills 2 cups.
The cups are the same shape and the same size.
Each cup holds the same amount of juice.
We have split the juice into 2 equal parts.
Each cup holds half of the bottle of juice.

Let's pour the juice from one of the
cups back into the bottle.

Look at the bottle.
Where is the top of the juice?
The bottle is half full of juice.

If we put the lid on the bottle and lay it on its
side it looks different. But it is still half full of juice.

PARENT AND TEACHER GUIDANCE

● Have children repeat the activity above using a 16-oz (480-ml) bottle and two 8-oz (250-ml) cups if possible, but note that the focus is on the concept of fractions rather than accurate measurement.

● Children need to see fractions in a variety of contexts. Encourage your child to explore halves and quarters in different ways, for example, halving a piece of food equally, splitting or grouping an even number of objects into halves or quarters, or using a balance scale to divide a piece of modeling dough into equal halves or quarters.

FRACTION FUN

Let's have some fun with fractions.

Find some containers in different sizes and shapes.

Fill half of each container with water.
Can you explain how you know it is half?

Let's find some halves.

pitcher

jam jar

plastic cup

yogurt pot

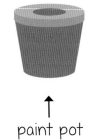
paint pot

PARENT AND TEACHER GUIDANCE

- Children will not be able to measure half of a volume accurately at this point, but games with water and different containers will give them experience in visualizing fractions.

HALF OF A LENGTH

You can find half the length of things such as ribbon, string, or paper by folding them so that the ends line up.

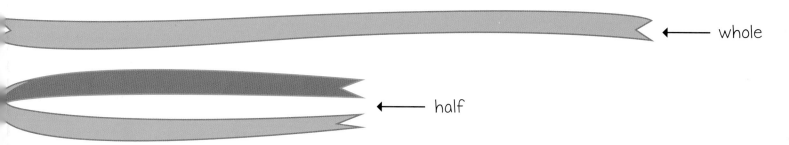

← whole

← half

Practice folding different-sized pieces of paper in half.

MAKING QUARTERS

We have found different ways to make a half,
now let's look at making the pieces even smaller.

A **quarter** is a smaller fraction than a half. When we want to
find a quarter of anything, we have to make 4 equal parts.
When we write a quarter in numbers, we write it like this: ¼

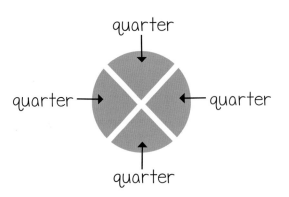

What is smaller than half of something?

We can cut a shape into 4 equal pieces.

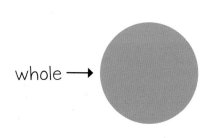

whole →

quarter

quarter → ✕ ← quarter

quarter

We can split a number of objects into 4 equal groups.

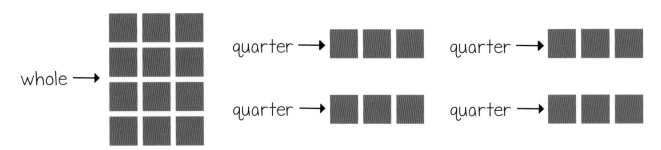

whole →

quarter →

quarter →

quarter →

quarter →

We can fill 4 cups with an equal amount of juice.

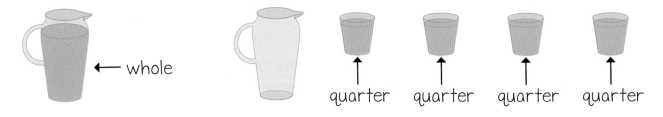

← whole

quarter   quarter   quarter   quarter

TRY THIS:
Which shapes have one quarter colored in?

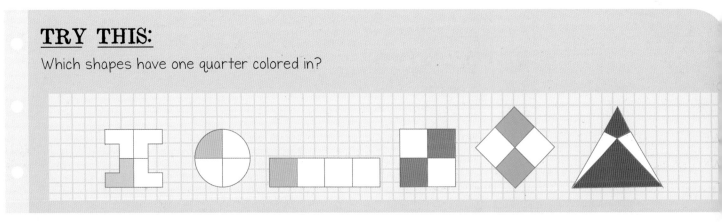

VOCABULARY: quarter

MODELING DOUGH FRACTIONS

Let's make some fractions using modeling dough.

YOU WILL NEED:

- modeling dough
- a rolling pin
- cookie cutters in different shapes
- a plastic knife

1. Roll out some modeling dough and use a cookie cutter to cut out a shape.

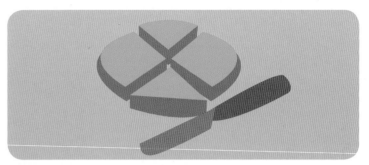

2. Use the plastic knife to cut your shape into 2 equal parts.
   What fractions have you made?

3. Make another modeling dough shape and cut it into 4 equal parts.
   What fractions have you made?

Make different modeling dough shapes and cut them into halves and quarters.

ODD AND EVEN

Let's think about half of a number.

Roll your modeling dough into 7 small balls.
Can you find half of the balls?
Remember, to find half, you need to divide the balls into 2 equal groups.

7 balls won't divide into 2 equal groups.
If we try to find half of 7, we get 2 groups of 3 and 1 left over.

We call numbers that don't divide into half exactly **odd** numbers.
We call numbers that do divide into half exactly **even** numbers.
Try dividing some different numbers in half to find out if they are odd or even.

VOCABULARY: odd, even

31

TOOLS FOR SUCCESS

Most of the math activities in the book can be carried out using everyday items, but the following mathematical tools are used in this book and you may find them useful.

Cubes

Cubes are perfect for teaching children counting, operations (addition, subtraction, multiplication, and division), place value, and early fractions. Sets of cubes that snap together are particularly useful.

Beads

Strings of beads can be used to recite number names in order from 0 to 20 or more, forward and backward. The color of beads can be varied every five beads to help children keep their place as they count.

Number line

A number line is a line with numbered points along it. The number line always has an arrow at each end to express the idea that it continues on infinitely. A number line can be used to count forward and back, to count on or back in different sized steps, to help children find one more, one less, and so on, as well as for understanding the basics of addition and subtraction.

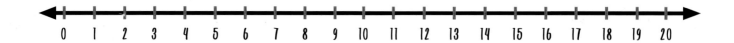

Number track

A number track shows numbers in order beginning at 1. Each space has a number in it. The numbers may be displayed on cards or on sticky notes or toys. A number track can be used in similar ways to a number line, but is particularly useful where numbers in the sequence can be masked or removed for finding missing numbers.

| 1 | 2 | 3 | 4 | 5 | 6 | 7 | 8 | 9 | 10 | 11 | 12 | 13 | 14 | 15 | 16 | 17 | 18 | 19 | 20 | 21 | 22 | 23 | 24 | 25 | 26 | 27 | 28 | 29 | 30 |

Ten-frame

A ten-frame is a two-by-five rectangular frame into which counters are placed to illustrate numbers less than or equal to ten. Several ten-frames can show numbers larger than ten. Using ten-frames can help children develop their understanding of the number ten and its key position in our number system. In their simplest form, ten-frames can be drawn on paper, but you could also create a box with ten compartments, for example by adapting an egg carton that contains 12 eggs.